The History of
Computers

Chris Oxlade

capstone

© 2018 Heinemann-Raintree
an imprint of Capstone Global Library, LLC
Chicago, Illinois

To contact Capstone Global Library please call 800-747-4992, or visit our website www.mycapstone.com

Edited by Helen Cox Cannons
Designed by Philippa Jenkins
Picture research by Svetlana Zhurkin
Production by Steve Walker
Originated by Capstone Global Library Ltd

Library of Congress Cataloging-in-Publication Data
Names: Oxlade, Chris, author.
Title: The history of computers / by Chris Oxlade.
Description: Chicaco, IL : Heinemann-Raintree, 2017. | Series: Heinemann
   first library. The history of technology | Includes bibliographical
   references and index. | Audience: Ages 7-11. | Audience: Grade 2 to Grade 5.
Identifiers: LCCN 2016058451 | ISBN 9781484640371 (library binding) | ISBN
   9781484640418 (pbk.) | ISBN 9781484640456 (ebook (pdf))
Subjects: LCSH: Computers–History–Juvenile literature.
Classification: LCC QA76.52 .O95 2017 | DDC 004–dc23
LC record available at https://lccn.loc.gov/2016058451

This book has been officially leveled by using the F&P Text Level Gradient ™ Leveling System

Acknowledgments
We would like to thank the following for permission to reproduce photographs: Getty Images: AFP/ Stan Honda, 21, Corbis/Charles O'Rear, 20, Future Publishing/Mark Madeo, 16, SSPL, 8, 9, 10; Newscom: Album/Oronoz, 6, Deutsch Presse Agentur/Lukas Barth, 22, EPA/Adam Warzawa, 17, ITAR-TASS/ Alexandra Mudrats, 26, Pries/Caro, 18, Reuters/Fred Prouser, 24, Reuters/Jeff Zelevansky, 27, Reuters/Mike Blake, 19, UIG/Underwood Archives, 12, 13, World History Archive, 7; Science Source: Eye of Science, 14; Shutterstock: Everett Historical, 11, HomeStudio, 4, padu_foto, 23, Rawpixel, 1, 5, robuart, 28, SpeedKingz, 25, Tinxi, 29, vectorfusionart, cover (right); SuperStock: age fotostock/Walter Bibikow, cover (left); Wikimedia: Thomas Nguyen, 15.

We would like to thank Matthew Anniss for his help in the preparation of this book.

Printed and Bound in China
PO4603

Table of Contents

Some words are shown in bold,
like this. You can find out what they
mean by looking in the glossary.

Computers were invented less than 100 years ago. Before this, there were machines that could add and subtract. One of these machines was the abacus. The abacus was invented more than 2,500 years ago.

On an abacus, counting was done using beads.

Children in schools use computers to help them learn.

Today, computers are everywhere. They are in homes, classrooms, and offices. They help us with daily jobs and allow us to keep in touch with each other. In addition to computers, there are also tablets and smartphones.

Before computers, there were **mechanical** calculating machines. In 1642, the French mathematician Blaise Pascal built a calculating machine. It used **cogs** and wheels to solve equations and record results.

Pascal's calculator was called the Pascaline.

Jacquard's loom was controlled by patterns of holes in cards.

In 1804, another Frenchman, Joseph-Marie Jacquard, built a **loom**. It could weave different patterns in cloth. Jacquard's loom was the first machine that could be programmed, just as computers are programmed to do different jobs.

Charles Babbage was an English inventor and mathematician. In the 1820s, Babbage designed an amazing **mechanical** calculator. He called it the Difference Engine. It had thousands of moving parts. However, Babbage never finished building it.

Babbage built part of his Difference Engine to test it.

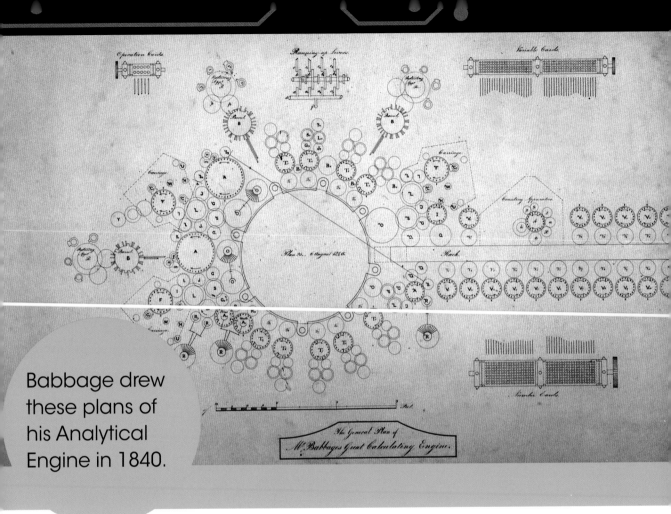

Babbage drew these plans of his Analytical Engine in 1840.

Babbage also designed and built a more **complicated** machine than the Difference Engine. It was called the **Analytical** Engine. The Analytical Engine was like a computer. But it became too expensive to finish.

Electronic Computers

Modern computers are **electronic** machines. They use very **complicated** electric **circuits** to store **data** and do calculations. The first electronic computers were built in the 1940s. They were big but less powerful than modern-day pocket calculators.

The Colossus computer helped to break German codes during World War II.

ENIAC filled a room 49 feet (15 meters) long and 30 feet (9 meters) wide.

In 1946, engineers in the United States finished building a computer. It was named the Electronic Numerical Integrator and Computer (ENIAC). It could do 5,000 calculations every second. This was incredible at the time. Like the Colossus computer, it was a huge machine.

Computers gradually got better. They could store more **data** and work faster. Their main job was to do calculations. This was called data processing. Two of the first office computers were the Ferranti Mark I and the UNIVAC I.

The UNIVAC I was made in 1951.

This was the first computer to be sold for office use.

By the end of the 1950s, many large businesses were using computers in their offices. The computers stored a lot of useful information, such as information about customers or about staff. Computers saved people time as they could find information quickly.

13

Two inventions allowed computers to become much smaller, faster, and cheaper to make. The first was the transistor. A transistor is a tiny **electronic** switch. The second invention was the **integrated circuit**. It was invented in 1958.

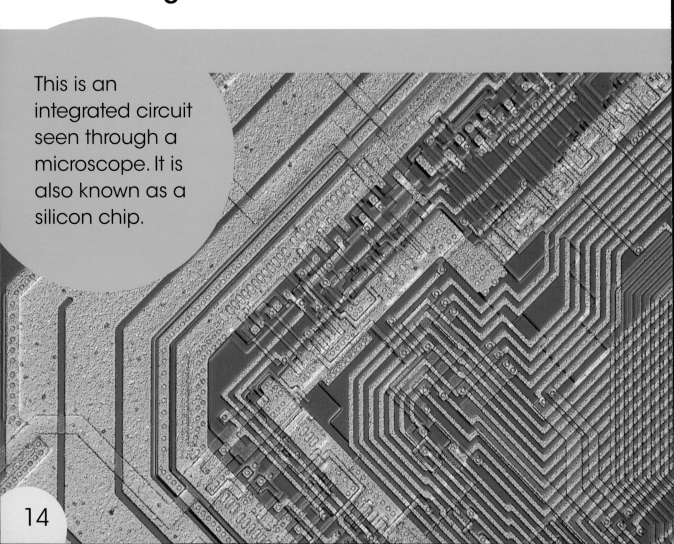

This is an integrated circuit seen through a microscope. It is also known as a silicon chip.

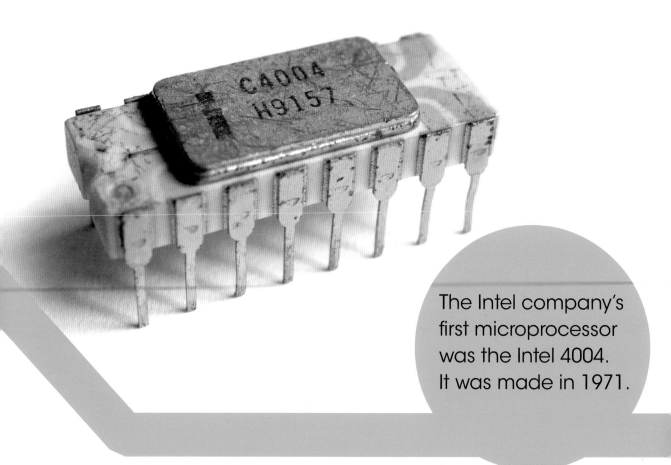

The Intel company's first microprocessor was the Intel 4004. It was made in 1971.

The next important moment in the history of computers was the invention of the microprocessor. This is also an integrated circuit. A microprocessor is the brains of a modern computer. It is the part of a computer that does calculations.

The first small home computer that people could buy was the Altair 8800. It came as a kit. People had to build it themselves. It allowed many people to try **programming** a computer for the first time.

The Altair 8800 of the 1970s had LEDs instead of a screen.

The Commodore 64 was the biggest selling computer during the 1980s.

Apple's first popular personal computer appeared in 1977. It was called the Apple II. In the 1980s, people could buy home computers that plugged into a television. Through them, people could have a go at **programming**.

In 1981, the computer company IBM released its first personal computer. It was called the IBM Personal Computer, or IBM PC. It was built using **software** called MS-DOS. This software was written by a small company named Microsoft. Half a million IBM PCs were sold in just two years.

This is one of the first IBM Personal Computers.

The Apple Macintosh was the first personal computer with on-screen windows.

Today, we use computers that show windows on a screen. We select things with a pointer that is controlled by a mouse or touchpad. This is called a graphical user interface (GUI). The first GUIs appeared in the 1980s.

Weather forecasters and other scientists use supercomputers to do calculations very quickly. The first supercomputer was the CDC 6600. It was built in 1964 and could do 3 million calculations per second. It was designed by Seymour Cray, an American **electronics** engineer.

The Cray-1 supercomputer was built in 1976.

Out of six games, Kasparov won three, drew two, and lost one to Deep Blue.

During the 1980s and 1990s, supercomputers got faster. Dozens of microprocessors worked together to do calculations. In 1996, a supercomputer called Deep Blue was programmed to play chess. It beat the world champion Gary Kasparov.

The first popular computer game was called Pong. It first appeared on **arcade game consoles** in 1972. From 1975, people could play Pong at home on the first Atari game console. The famous game Space Invaders appeared in arcades in 1978.

Pong was a simple bat-and-ball game.

The original Nintendo Game Boy was first sold in 1989.

In the 1980s and 1990s, home game consoles quickly became more powerful. Handheld game consoles such as the Nintendo Game Boy also became popular. The PlayStation 1 was released in 1995, and the first Xbox in 2001.

23

A network is made up of computers linked to each other. They share information. The Internet connects millions of computers around the world. It started in the 1970s. At first, it was used by scientists in the U.S. and Europe. They used it to swap information.

On October 29, 1969, this machine sent the very first message on the Internet.

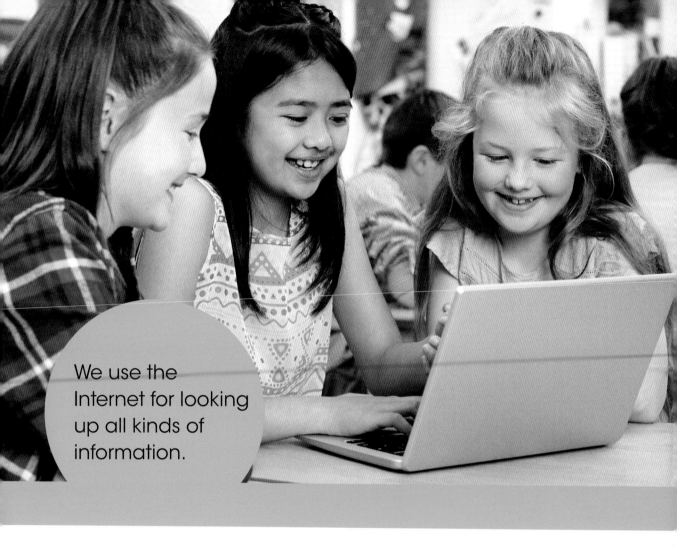

We use the Internet for looking up all kinds of information.

By the 1990s, anyone with a telephone line and a computer could connect to the Internet. Today, we use the Internet to send emails and **browse** web pages. We can connect to the Internet using **Wi-Fi** and through the mobile telephone network.

25

The idea of a tablet is not new. The first tablet **device** was the Apple Newton MessagePad. It could handle emails, act as a diary, a calculator, and a simple **word processor**. Devices like this were known as personal digital assistants (PDAs).

Apple's Newton was first sold in 1993.

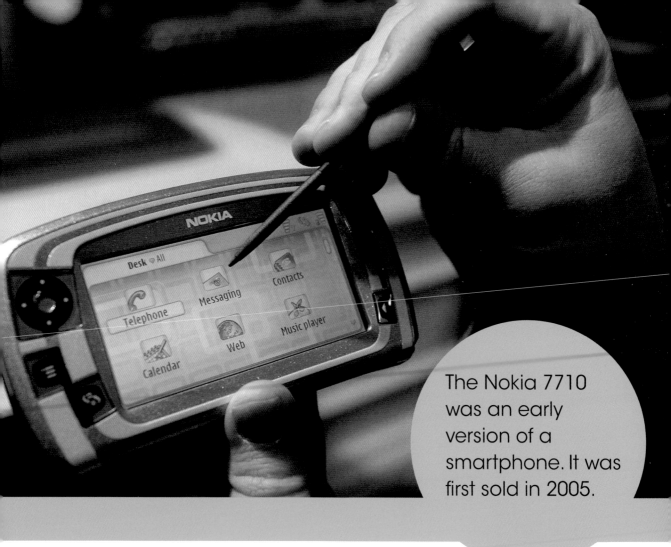

The Nokia 7710 was an early version of a smartphone. It was first sold in 2005.

A smartphone is a cross between a phone and a computer. The first smartphones appeared in the 1990s. They had larger screens than normal mobile telephones and small keyboards. Later, they also included cameras.

It is hard to know what computers will be like in the future. But we can be sure that computers will be able to do more **complicated** jobs for us. All our **data** will probably be stored on the Internet instead of on computers. This is called cloud computing.

The place where Internet data is stored is called "The Cloud."

CLOUD
storage

A virtual reality headset shows us images in 3D.

The way we control computers in the future will also change. We might use hand gestures, such as waving. We may also use our eyes to control computers. **Virtual reality** headsets or transparent displays might replace normal computer screens.

Glossary

arcade—an amusement center with coin-operated games

browse—to look at words, pictures, and videos on a website

circuit—a loop that electricity flows around

cog—a wheel with teeth around the edge

complicated—having lots of different parts

data—information stored on a computer

device—electronic equipment made for doing a certain job

electronics—electric circuits that do complicated jobs for us

game console—a machine for playing computer games on

integrated circuit—a small piece of material with a tiny electric circuit built on it

loom—a machine that weaves yarn or thread into cloth

mechanical—operated by a machine or machinery

programming—writing a list of instructions for a computer to follow

software—instructions within a computer's memory that tell the computer what to do

virtual reality—realistic 3D world drawn by a computer that can be seen using a special headset

Wi-Fi—a way of connecting computers in the same area without using wires

word processor—a computer that is used to write words, sentences, and paragraphs

Read More

Beascoa, Santiago. *Then & Now: A Journey Through the History of Machines*. New York: Sterling Children's Books, 2016.

Hubbard, Ben. *How Computers Work*. Our Digital Planet. North Mankato, Minn.: Heinemann Raintree, 2017.

Yearling, Tricia. *Computers: What They Are and How to Use Them*. Zoom in on Technology. New York: Enslow Publishing, 2016.

Internet Sites

FactHound offers a safe, fun way to find Internet sites related to this book. All of the sites on FactHound have been researched by our staff.

Here's all you do:

Visit *www.facthound.com*

Type in this code: 9781484640371

Index